THE BHOPAL
CHEMICAL LEAK

These and other titles are available in the
Lucent World Disasters Series:

THE BHOPAL CHEMICAL LEAK

by
Arthur Diamond

Illustrations by
Brian McGovern

LUCENT
B·O·O·K·S

WORLD DISASTERS

The author would like to thank Dan Kurzman for capturing the stories that might have escaped untold.

Library of Congress Cataloging-in-Publication Data

Diamond, Arthur, 1957-
    The Bhopal chemical leak / by Arthur Diamond.
        p. cm. — (World disasters)
    Includes bibliographical references.
    Summary: Examines the chemical leak at Bhopal in its historical, cultural, and human contexts.
    ISBN 1-56006-009-3
    1. Bhopal Union Carbide Plant Disaster, Bhopal, India, 1984—Juvenile literature. 2. Chemical industry—Accidents—Environmental aspects—India—Bhopal—Juvenile literature. 3. Methyl isocyanate—Toxicology—India—Bhopal—Juvenile literature. [1. Bhopal Union Carbide Plant Disaster, Bhopal, India, 1984. 2. Chemical industry—Accidents.] I. Title.
HD7269.C452I5234 1990
363.17'91'09543—dc20   90-6011
                                                         CIP
                                                          AC

© Copyright 1990 by Lucent Books, Inc.
Lucent Books, Inc., P.O. Box 289011, San Diego, California, 92198-0011

To Raj Kumar Keswani

Table of Contents

Preface
The World Disasters Series

World disasters have always aroused human curiosity. Whenever news of tragedy spreads, we want to learn more about it. We wonder how and why the disaster happened, how people reacted, and whether we might have acted differently. To be sure, disaster evokes a wide range of responses—fear, sorrow, despair, generosity, even hope. Yet from every great disaster, one remarkable truth always seems to emerge: in spite of death, pain, and destruction, the human spirit triumphs.

History is full of disasters, arising from a variety of causes. Earthquakes, floods, volcanic eruptions, and other natural events often produce widespread destruction. Just as often, however, people accidentally bring suffering and distress on themselves and other human beings. And many disasters have sinister causes, like human greed, envy, or prejudice.

The disasters included in this series have been chosen not only for their dramatic qualities, but also for their educational value. The reader will learn about the causes and effects of the greatest disasters in history. Technical concepts and interesting anecdotes are explained and illustrated in inset boxes.

But disasters should not be viewed in isolation. To enrich the reader's understanding, these books present historical information about the time period, and interesting facts about the culture in which each disaster occurred. Finally, they teach valuable lessons about human nature. More acts of bravery, cowardice, intelligence, and foolishness are compressed into the few days of a disaster than most people experience in a lifetime.

Dramatic illustrations and evocative narrative lure the reader to distant cities and times gone by. Readers witness the awesome power of an exploding volcano, the magnitude of a violent earthquake, and the hopelessness of passengers on a mighty ship passing to its watery grave. By reliving the events, the reader will see how disaster affects the lives of real people and will gain a deeper understanding of their sorrow, their pain, their courage, and their hope.

Introduction

Wind-Borne Death

One fateful night in December 1984, an explosion in the Union Carbide chemical plant in Bhopal, India, unleashed a deadly gas called methyl isocyanate, or MIC, used to make pesticides. The gas cloud left an estimated 8,000 people dead and about 300,000 more suffering from its effects. These victims had no warning about what was to happen.

Lives were spared or snuffed out in minutes. Some of the fortunate residents rounded up their families and ran across the path of the wind and away from the direction in which it was blowing. In this way, many people unknowingly saved their lives. Others were not as lucky. They headed north, toward the chemical plant, right into the deadly cloud. Many also ran south, but the wind caught up with them.

At daybreak, relief workers wandering through the city discovered the devastation the deadly gas had caused. Bloated carcasses of cattle dotted the streets. Tree and plant leaves were yellow and brittle. Corpses littered the streets as well

The Bhopal Chemical Leak in History

2500 B.C.
Beginning of the Indus Valley Civilization, the oldest in India and one of the oldest in the world.

1500 B.C.
The Aryan race invades India and establishes a great civilization that develops classical Indian culture based on the caste system and the Vedic (Hindu) religion.

500 B.C.
Siddhartha Guatama, The Buddha, confronts the established religious doctrines of the day and teaches his followers a new way to find eternal salvation, known in the West as Buddhism.

273 B.C.
Asoka, grandson of Chandragupta, unites almost the entire Indian subcontinent for the first time under one ruler. He declares Buddhism the state religion.

A.D. 1192
The first Muslim kingdom is established in India after centuries of Muslim raids and battles with Hindu nations.

1498
Portuguese explorer Vasco da Gama is the first European to land in India.

1526
Babar, a Muslim conqueror, establishes the Mogul empire, later consolidated by the great Akbar.

1757
The beginning of the British empire in India.

1914-1918
World War I weakens British rule in India.

1919
Mohandas K. Gandhi organizes his first nonviolent protest against British abuses.

1939-1945
World War II.

and were discovered behind locked doors, trapped in private death tombs.

The Bhopal disaster ranks as one of the worst industrial accidents of all time. This is true not only because a great number of lives were lost but because the injuries to survivors and the effects on generations to come were serious and long-lasting. Survivors have developed disorders in their central nervous systems, in their hearts, and in their kidneys. Doctors and scientists fear genetic damage in the children of survivors.

When Bhopal welcomed Union Carbide's chemical plant to its northern city limits in 1969, people looked forward to a bright future. With the plant would come jobs, and with jobs, prosperity. Both the Indian government and Union Carbide hoped that the Bhopal plant would breathe new life into the capital city at the very center of India. Instead, the stricken plant brought death.

Perhaps the most tragic aspect of the disaster is that the deaths might have been avoided completely. For, as in many such disasters, human greed, negligence, and inattention played a large role. For this reason, the story of Bhopal should not be forgotten.

1947
India gains independence from British rule and is divided into (Hindu) India and (Muslim) Pakistan.

1948
Gandhi is assassinated by a religious fanatic.

1950
A thirty-thousand-square-mile earthquake kills at least twenty thousand people in India's state of Assam.

1965
India and Pakistan go to war over which owns the territory of Kashmir.

1971
East Pakistan declares independence from Pakistan; becomes Bangladesh.

1974
India tests its first atomic bomb.

1984
Indian Prime Minister Indira Gandhi is assassinated by Sikh gunmen.

A Union Carbide chemical plant in Bhopal explodes, spewing toxic gases into the surrounding area; 2000 people die, more than 100,000 are injured.

1988
Benazir Bhutto becomes the first woman to be chosen prime minister of Pakistan.

One

A Lively City

Bhopal is the capital of the state of Madhya Pradesh, which is located at the center of India. Madhya Pradesh is mostly a jungle region with fifty-five million people. The average income throughout this state is very low, as it is for most people in India.

India occupies a triangular land mass ranging from the Himalaya Mountains in the north, down to the Indian Ocean at the bottom tip. It shares the triangular Indian subcontinent with Pakistan, Nepal, Bhutan, and Bangladesh. This vast land mass possesses an almost endless variety of climates and vegetation. The Himalaya Mountains, highest in the world, stretch across India's northern borders. Below them stretches the Ganges Plain, which is wide, fertile, and densely populated. The Indian continent

also includes lush jungles and dry, hot deserts. The climate varies from tropical heat in the south to near-arctic cold in the North Rajasthan Desert in the northwest.

Greatly overpopulated, India in 1983 contained more than 730 million people, and the number grows by an estimated 1 million people a month. The population is expected to reach 1 billion by the year 2000. This huge population means that much of India does not have the resources to meet the daily needs of its people. As a result, most of the country is plagued by desperate poverty. Bhopal is no exception.

Seen from a distance, the city of Bhopal spreads randomly among low, rolling hills and valleys. To the south of the city are two shimmering lakes that supply Bhopal's water. The lakes and the gentle hills separate the various townships from Old Bhopal in the north of the city and from each other. In this city of 900,000 people, single-story houses sprawl in all directions.

Always Crowded

At one end of the city is the railway station, which is always crowded with people. The station's stifling air is filled with dust and the smells of car exhaust and dung. Outside the building, commuters argue loudly for the privilege of hiring battered taxis, and horse-pulled carts transport crowds of swaying people and wide-eyed babies. Motorcycles and bicycles carry

entire families. Cage-carts, drawn by bicycles, are crammed with schoolchildren on their way to lessons. Seven to ten people may ride in one car. Most people, however, walk, mingling with the communities of people who make the streets their home.

Many people crowd the railway station every day. Most are visitors, planning to meet with government officials, to shop, or to visit relatives. Wage earners also fill the station, taking trains to other cities in hopes that they can earn a few rupees elsewhere. In addition, newcomers arrive daily at the station from rural villages and seek the jobs they believe to be available in a big city like Bhopal.

Everywhere in Bhopal, religion is evident, and the railway station is no exception. Here, departing Hindus may be spotted, offering prayers to their gods for a safe trip. They leave religious paintings, created with chalk, powder, and rose petals, on the floor of the station. Eighty percent of Indians are adherents of Hinduism, one of the world's great religions. For the Hindu, life is an illusion. Death is not to be feared, because a Hindu believes he or she will be reincarnated, or returned to life. Hindus believe that the souls of people and animals pass into new bodies of the same or different species as punishment or reward for previous actions. This idea is called the doc-

A HUGE NATION OF SMALL VILLAGES

Villages are the roots of India—there are almost 600,000 of them. Villagers still make up more than seven-tenths of the entire population of India. Many villagers have left their homes for the job opportunities they hope to find in India's cities, like Bhopal. Nearly half of Bhopal's population of 900,000 has drifted in from the villages.

In the villages, the literacy rate is low. Only one woman in four and half the men can read. Though India's constitution provides for the education of all people up to the age of fourteen, this goal is far from being met. A common sight in a village in India is to see a boy or young man who can read quoting from a newspaper or magazine to a small group around him. This young villager may be the first in his family to have learned to read.

trine of the Transmigration of Souls.

Although Hinduism is the country's leading religion, the majority of Bhopal's residents are Muslims. Muslims are adherents of Islam, which in Arabic means "submission to God." Public worship takes place in mosques, which are often highly decorated temples with colorfully patterned tiles. One of the biggest mosques in the world, the Taj-ul-Masajid, is near Lower Lake, south of the city. Five times every day, Bhopal's Muslims are called to pray at this and other numerous mosques around the city. Comprising about 80 million people out of the total Indian population of 730 million, Muslims have always been in conflict with the Hindu majority. Their feuds began over one thousand years ago when Muslim in-

vaders first came to India, and struggles continue today throughout the crowded country.

Just a few footsteps from the railway station is Old Bhopal. Gathered around an area called Jama Masjid, Old Bhopal was a walled fort in ancient times, and some of the wall still remains. The neighborhood's winding, narrow streets suffer from overcrowding and congestion. Shops and businesses line the streets. Tailors, squatting in alcoves barely big enough to cross their legs in, do a good business sewing dhotis and saris, common pieces of Indian clothing. Metalworkers in the back rooms of shops are busy at their crafts. Sidewalk barbers lather the faces of impatient customers.

Food is sold everywhere in Old Bhopal. Egg vendors prepare omelets at curbside stands. The smell of fish mixes with the aroma of tea and spices. Sugar cane is crushed and sold as a drink. A charity food-stall dishes out lentils and rice to the poor. In tiny restaurants, un-leavened bread, thick lentil soup, and chicken cooked with curry are enjoyed. Rice and fish dishes are staples, and the standard beverage is tea, to which people sometimes add butter made from goat's milk and a dash of salt.

Three Main Classes of People

In Bhopal, as in all of India, there are three main classes of people: top, middle, and bottom. The top class includes managers and officials who work in government and indus-try, wealthy businessmen, engineers, doctors, and other professionals. They live in a new section of the city, with paved streets, larger apart-ments, and rare amenities like air-conditioning. They also live in the city's new and modern colonies, cre-ated especially for them, a good dis-tance to the south and west of crowded Old Bhopal. Bhopal's mid-dle class is composed of business-men, artisans, and lower manage-ment and government officials. They live and work throughout the city. Though they may hold vital jobs, their incomes are low and their benefits are poor. Government offi-cials work in offices without tele-phones and typewriters. (It has been estimated that there is only one telephone per one thousand people in India.) Government in-spectors are usually ill-equipped to

THE LAKES OF BHOPAL

Walking south from the railway sta-tion and Old Bhopal, one would pass the cinema house, Maulana Azad Central Library, the vegetable market, and Sultania Hospital before arriving at Lower Lake. The larger Upper Lake is just to the west, with Hamidia Hospital on its northern shore.

Bhopal residents are proud of their lakes. *"Tal to Bhopal tal our sab ta-laiya hain"* is a popular expression in Bhopal; it means "only Bhopal lakes are the lakes; others are simply ponds."

About twenty-three million gallons of water are pumped each day from huge Upper Lake, the city's main wa-ter supply. The water has to be boiled to kill viruses that may have escaped the city's filtration system. Upper Lake has a yacht club—for the few who can afford to use it—on its southern shore.

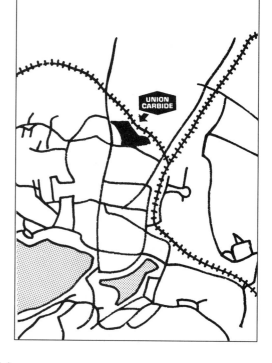

do their jobs—for example, in years past the air and water control board did not have a single instrument for measuring air pollution.

Jobs Are Halved and Quartered

Because of the overwhelming number of people in need of work, the relatively few jobs in Bhopal are halved and quartered. For example, if you tried to buy a shirt in Bhopal, you would be in for quite an adventure. One man would fit you, another would wrap the shirt, another would take your money, another would give you your change and receipt, and perhaps another would bang a stamp to officially record the event at the very end. Although this division of labor may seem extremely strange to us, in a country such as India, even a meager, low-paying job is welcomed as a way to avoid abject poverty.

Workers in the bottom class of society take any job they can find. If they are fortunate, they may be employed in the glue factory, the bone mills, the tannery center, the distillery, the slaughterhouse, the straw products factory, or other small industries around the city. Otherwise, these people work as sidewalk vendors who shine shoes, give haircuts, or clean ears. They find jobs as street cleaners or in communal sewing centers. In Old Bhopal, some workers ladle treated lake water to thirsty citizens.

In addition to these unofficial social classes, Hindus in Bhopal and throughout India adhere to a rigid caste system that further separates people into classes. This system is ancient, dating back to 3000 B.C. Though legislation has tried to abolish it, the caste system endures. It divides people in Hindu society primarily according to their ancestry, occupation, and skin color. There are four main classes: Brahman (priest); Kshatriya (warrior); Vaisya (merchant or farmer); and Sudra (menial labor). A recent addition is the category of Outvarnas, or untouchables. People relegated to this caste are abhorred by Hindus of other castes. Untouchables perform jobs such as garbage collection and burying the dead.

While cities such as Bhopal are less rigid regarding caste, rural people insist on enforcing these ancient rules. For example, in the vil-

---

THE EXTENDED FAMILY

In crowded India, most people live in extended families. A large family makes economic sense: the more members there are, the more hands there are available to work. Even if they have a meager income, a couple and their children often share their home with brothers and sisters, parents, grandparents, uncles, and aunts. In India, children take care of their aged parents.

In society and in their families women are traditionally treated as second-class citizens in India. Economic necessity, though, often wins out and changes this tradition. For example, a widow is usually forced by her family to live a life of seclusion, but if the widow is the breadwinner, she can become the head of the household. Usually, there are only one or two wage earners in an entire household.

THE CASTE SYSTEM

The caste system has served to order Indian society into classes, primarily by categorizing people at birth, although religion and occupation are also considered. The caste system in India dates back to 3000 B.C. The system is outlawed today but flourishes nevertheless. It consists of four main *varnas*, or classes, in which there are many subclasses—between three and four thousand in the whole of India. This system is so complicated that an average Indian does not fully understand the complexities of the various subclasses. The four main classes are the Brahmans, the scholars and intellectuals; the Kshatriyas, the warriors, kings and fighters who defended the country; the Vaisyas, the merchants, traders, bankers, and other businessmen; and the Sudras, the agricultural laborers. A fifth class, the Outvarnas, or untouchables, was created later. These people perform the very lowest tasks in society, such as emptying lavatories, mending shoes, and cremating the dead.

lages of India, one from a higher caste may not shop, dine, have tea, or even converse with someone from a lower caste.

In theory, one cannot change caste. In practice, though, through effort, talent, and luck, one may change caste by gaining prominence in a certain occupation. In village life, politics, and in marriage, however, the caste system offers little flexibility. Even in modern cities today, Indians do not accept the marriage of a Brahman and an untouchable.

Only Hindus Have Caste

Religion plays a major role in the caste system. Only Hindus can have caste, leaving people belonging to minority religions like Islam, Buddhism, Jainism, and Sikhism altogether outside the system. This is why many lower-caste Indians convert to Islam—in order to escape their rigid station in life.

In Bhopal, the lower-caste poor, usually unemployed, live in slum colonies and shantytowns in areas like Chola, north of Old Bhopal. Chola is one of the largest slum colonies in Bhopal and is ringed by shantytowns that are populated mostly by squatters. These squatters live in huts and shacks made of mud, boards, and cow dung. The better huts have makeshift tin roofs to protect dwellers from the occasional rain. While women wash rags and dishes at communal street pools, men stand in front of their huts, gossiping and smoking home-made cigarettes called *bidis*. Along the rubble-strewn main streets, vendors push fly-infested carts of vegetables and fruits.

Scrawny dogs and goats wander from hut to hut, nibbling at refuse. The smell of garbage, as well as the stench of animal and human excrement, pervades the air. For bedding, families sleep on sweat-stained mats and cots. Their goats and dogs sleep in the huts with them.

In the midst of the poverty and chaos of Bhopal, Union Carbide opened its chemical plant in 1969. Located at the city limits about a mile northwest of the railway station, the new plant served as the northern boundary of Chola and its neighboring slum colony to the west, Jai Prakash Nagar. Immediately, additional shantytowns sprang up right across the street from the new plant. Arriving squatters wanted to be as close to the plant as possible. They would have lived inside the grounds, if they could have. For these people, the new plant represented the possibility of a job. They hoped to work either inside the plant or at one of the industries or shops they believed the plant would attract. In their desperate condition, the people of Bhopal were not concerned about the safety of the chemicals produced at the plant.

Two

Jobs First, Safety Last

Union Carbide was first incorporated in India in 1940, when it began producing batteries in Calcutta. From that time on, the corporation gradually became a fixture in India, producing primarily batteries and flashlights. By the late 1960s, thirteen Union Carbide chemical plants dotted the Indian landscape. Union Carbide India, Limited (UCIL), became one of the largest companies in all of India, employing more than ten thousand people, of which one thousand earned 3,000 rupees ($250) per month—a very high salary for any Indian worker. In 1969, Bhopal welcomed India's fourteenth Union Carbide chemical plant, built on eighty acres of land on the northern edge of the city.

In the early 1970s, the Bhopal plant imported, packaged, and distributed pesticides and raw fertilizers for use in India and East Asia. In 1980, though, wanting to expand its business and trim costs, Union Carbide decided to manufacture pesticides at the Bhopal plant. This meant that deadly chemicals would be produced and mixed on the premises.

Many local Indian leaders objected to the new plan. They pointed out that any chemical accident could immediately poison the large population living in the slums around the plant. They also noted that the plant was only a couple of miles away from Old Bhopal and the busy railway station. They argued that if an accident occurred, it could threaten the lives of thousands. The leaders advised that the chemical-producing unit be established far out in the northeast sector of the city. They also urged further investigations into the dangers that might be posed by the plant.

Union Carbide Too Powerful

But Union Carbide was too powerful and influential to be defeated, and the objections of the local leaders were overruled. Union Carbide did not want to relocate the plant to a less-populated area. As a result, the new insecticide-production unit was built in the existing plant as planned.

This pleased the majority of Bhopal's residents, who did not really care about what was produced at the plant. Sayed Abbas, for example, saw a great future in the industry and technology that

18

the plant offered.

Abbas, a television repairman, believed that Union Carbide would be good for his business. More people with jobs meant that more televisions would be bought. He had moved his family from city to city, finally settling in Bhopal because of the business opportunities he believed to exist there. He had a lot of experience with televisions and hoped to eventually open a repair shop in Bhopal.

Though finding work in the city was sometimes difficult, Abbas, a devout Muslim, was driven to succeed. He had to support his wife, four daughters, two sons, and his ailing mother. This meant that he would often travel far from his home by train to outlying villages to service television sets. Abbas was like many people living in Bhopal, working a variety of jobs to make ends meet. Abbas was not the only person who believed the factory was a sign of opportunity.

Chandabee came to Bhopal with her husband, her two daughters, and her mother-in-law. She belonged to one of India's aboriginal tribes and left the plains and jungles of the state of Madhya Pradesh for the opportunities in Bhopal. For several reasons, tribal people are considered the lowest of the lowest caste—even lower than the untouchables—by other Indians. One reason is that because of their fear of doctors and modern medicine, diseases such as cholera, syphilis, gonorrhea, tuberculosis,

malaria, and skin ailments are epidemic among tribal people.

Chandabee was especially concerned about her health because she was pregnant. Though often reduced to begging, Chandabee, a musician, tried hard to find entertainment jobs in Bhopal. Her husband found work cleaning streets or digging ditches. Chandabee and her family lived in a hut across from the Union Carbide plant. There, in the shadow of the plant's smokestack, Chandabee could dream about the future.

Munnibai Balkishensingh could see the smokestack of the Union Carbide plant every day during work at the railway station, in Old Bhopal, about a mile south of the plant. Munnibai was very grateful for her job at the station. She inherited the job when her husband died in 1972. Munnibai would sit on a bench until a train pulled into the station or was about to leave. Her job was to stay in a small stall by the side of the tracks and ladle water out of a pail for the train passengers. She wore an official sari, which was white with blue borders. Earning more than a common laborer, she was happy with her job. Her two sons studied at a free public school, and the rest of the family was unable to find work. They all depended on Munnibai's salary to keep them alive.

Munnibai had originally come to Bhopal from a neighboring village with her husband. She lived in a mud hut fashioned out of a small hill near the tracks of the station. She shared this dark, two-room structure with her two sons, a widowed daughter with three children,

21

a second daughter, and a brother-in-law.

Munnibai worried about her eldest son's grades in school. Lately, he had not been doing too well. She hoped that he would succeed and make their family proud by rising out of their caste. Seeing the smoke from the Union Carbide plant smokestack nearby made her feel sad. To her, the smoke was a symbol of the success and prosperity her eldest son might never reach.

Many Bhopal residents shared the hopes of Munnibai, Abbas, and Chandabee about the Union Carbide plant. The tremendous poverty, joblessness, and strife that are rampant throughout most of India force its citizens to see opportunity in any new business venture. Unfortunately, this hope and trust were sadly misplaced in the Union Carbide plant.

Worker Dies in First Year

In December 1981, the first year of pesticide production at the Bhopal plant, a worker died. Ashrat Mohammed Khan died within a day of being drenched with a deadly gas when he was cleaning a pipe. Three other workers were injured in the same accident, involving a deadly chemical called methyl isocyanate (MIC). MIC is one of the ingredients of Union Carbide's popular pesticide SEVIN. In the Bhopal plant, three tanks held more than forty-six tons of the deadly chemical.

Even before beginning production of chemicals, the Bhopal

plant's safety record was suspect. Since the plant's opening in 1969, there had been six accidents. In 1979, an American safety team from Union Carbide came to Bhopal. They did not like the current safety program and suggested that a plan for alerting citizens in case of a spill be drawn up. But local officials were never told of this. Then in 1980, a Union Carbide safety expert arrived from the United States and repeated what the previous experts had said: Devise an evacuation plan. Again, local officials were apparently never notified. While it is not certain why Union Carbide kept these recommendations secret, some experts believe that the company was afraid that local leaders would panic and shut down the plant.

Experts Send Warning

In mid-1982, another team of American experts sent a report to Bhopal, warning of the danger of a major chemical reaction inside one of the chemical storage tanks. The report made safety suggestions, all of which, except for one, were implemented, and the experts left, satisfied. Though a few small leaks

MULTINATIONAL CORPORATIONS ARE WELCOMED

Developing countries all over the world welcome multinational corporations. These huge corporations provide jobs and essential products for poor people, and the multinationals benefit from locating their plants in a Third World country, where labor and operating costs are low. But multinationals have become a controversial topic, as critics point out some disadvantages. Several well-publicized cases have revealed that these companies may take advantage of the poverty and ignorance of the native people. One example of this type of exploitation has been the production of hazardous substances under low safety standards in poor host countries. Because multinationals often find themselves with more money than the host government, it is easy for them to influence these governments to help their business activities, which often do not put a high priority on plant safety. Union Carbide, in Bhopal, was one of these companies.

developed in the two years following this report, the plant managers were not too worried. They believed that the risk of a major leak was low.

The 1982 inspection report also identified serious problems in the design of the Bhopal plant. One problem was the backup system that was to be used in case of a mechanical failure. For instance, if a pump failed, a backup pump would take over. The danger with the Bhopal plant's backup system was that it was manual, which meant that a malfunction or accident had to be identified by a worker who would then start the backup. Though much less efficient, the manual system was favored for use in the Bhopal plant because it provided more jobs. The safest backup systems, however, were automatic. These were commonly used in plants in Europe and the United States and even in an identical plant in West Virginia.

Other factors influenced the safety of the plant. Since 1981, business had not been good for Union Carbide. Due to rising prices, the company's expensive pesticides were being ignored by much of India's population, who had begun to seek cheaper, local pesticides. Also, pesticide use had declined all over the world because of widespread ecological problems, including harm to people, wildlife, and water supplies.

According to many workers, Union Carbide's economic problems affected safety procedures. Workers were ordered to be less diligent about quality control. Instead of replacing leaky pipes, the workers—many of whom were underqualified for their positions—were told to patch them.

In response to these conditions,

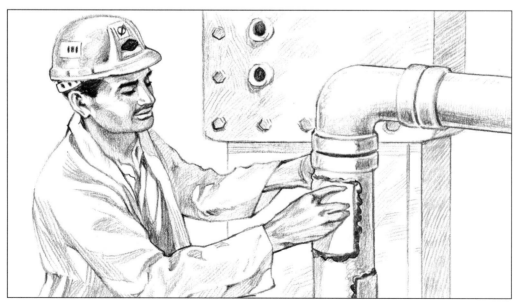

PESTICIDES

Since the beginning of history, people have been trying to increase the amount of food they produce. This most often takes the form of a battle against bugs. Insects destroy one-third of all crops every year. To combat these bugs, people have developed and continue to develop pesticides. In Bhopal, the word *pesticide* is translated to mean "medicine for food."

Pesticides are substances that kill plants or animals that damage crops or endanger the well-being of man and selected animals. There are four basic types of pesticides: herbicides, which kill plants; fungicides, which kill fungi; rodenticides, which kill mice and rats; and insecticides, which kill insects.

People stand outside the Union Carbide plant in Bhopal, India. In 1984, two of the largest slum colonies were located right across the street from the plant.

two plant labor unions protested and staged a hunger strike in 1982. All of the workers were fired by Union Carbide, and the protest was quickly forgotten.

Serious accidents continued to occur at the plant. From 1981 to 1984, eighteen more workers were exposed to deadly chemicals, including MIC. By 1984, forty-seven people had been injured at the plant and over $620,000 worth of property destroyed.

Accidents Are Ignored

These accidents went largely ignored by the people of Bhopal. A local journalist named Raj Kumar Keswani, however, provided a steady supply of reports about the safety problems at Union Carbide.

Keswani first became interested in the new chemical-production unit after talking to a friend in 1982. The friend used to work at the plant but quit because he thought it was not safe enough. Keswani was driven to discover more about the plant. At first, his evidence seemed to confirm what everyone believed— that Union Carbide had a spotless reputation in India as well as in the United States.

But then he discovered some negative aspects of Union Car-bide's Indian operations. Beginning with a 1982 newspaper article, Keswani published warnings about the potential for disaster at the Bhopal plant. He asserted that the workers were not trained well, and he pointed out the flaws in the manual backup system. He also drew attention to the alarming proximity of the slum colonies to the plant.

Few people in Bhopal took the journalist's warnings seriously. Keswani went on to write two more articles in the next two years questioning the plant's safety, but he was frustrated each time by the general apathy of the people of Bhopal and its government officials. Keswani even wrote to the chief minister of the state but received no reply.

In December 1984, more than 130,000 people—20 percent of the city's population—lived in the slum colonies and shantytowns of Bhopal. The two largest slum colonies, Chola and Jai Prakash Nagar, were right across the street from the Union Carbide plant. In 1984, Keswani warned that the next time the Union Carbide factory leaked, "there will not even be a solitary witness to testify to what took place."

Three

A City Gasps

On December 2, 1984, at about 11:00 P.M., the technicians in the Union Carbide plant gathered in their control room for a tea break. Minutes earlier, they had noticed some drops of yellowish white gas fifty feet above the floor in the room where the deadly pesticide MIC was stored. Some of the men wanted to make sure the liquid was not a pesticide leak from one of the tanks. But others were convinced it could wait—what could possibly be dangerous or pressing about a tiny leak? The technicians decided to attend to the curious liquid after they had their tea.

When it was time to get back to work, all but a few of the technicians stepped through the door of the control room and into the main area. Suddenly, they fell, coughing and retching, to their hands and knees. They understood now that

something terrible had gone wrong. They wiped furiously at their burning eyes. They climbed up on top of the tanks to get closer to the area where they had seen the leak, but it was now too late. The gas was deadly MIC. Inside tank No. 610, which was covered by a sixty-foot long, six-inch thick cement slab, the pesticide had begun to boil. The technicians could hear it bubbling and felt tremendous pressure underfoot. The technicians in the main area all ran for their lives, and the great slab of concrete, now hot to the touch, cracked open, letting deadly fumes escape.

Technicians Alerted

Back in the control room, the remaining technicians who had viewed the scene in the main area alerted other technicians and acted fast to try to contain the gas. There were five major backup systems they could use to either neutralize or contain the escaping MIC. First, they called in the company fire trucks to spray and neutralize the gas. But the spray from the hoses could not travel high enough to reach the gas. Second, technicians tried using the vent gas scrubber pump. The vent gas scrubber would take the escaping gas and "scrub," or neutralize, it with a caustic soda solution. The technicians knew, though, that the scrubber pump had not been tried since it was recently repaired. They turned on the power—nothing happened. The pump was either defective or out of

the caustic soda solution.

Next, the technicians thought of transferring the liquid in tank No. 610 to a nearby tank, always kept empty in case of an emergency. But MIC had already been transferred to the empty tank just a few days before. The technicians were afraid that if they transferred additional MIC into the standing MIC, it would cause a chemical reaction that could possibly compound the disaster. They noted that reactions had already begun in the second tank and pressure had started to build. They immediately rejected the transfer option. Some technicians wondered if they could cool the liquid in tank No. 610 with the refrigeration unit. But the unit had been shut down five months ago,

when production of the pesticide had stopped. There was no time to get it up and running. The last backup device was the flame tower. This was a ninety-foot high pipe used to burn gases in the air. It was supposed to be burning twenty-four hours a day. But it was being repaired. Frustrated and frightened, the technicians sounded an alarm and ran for their lives. There was nothing they could do to prevent the deadly gas from drifting up and out into the chilly Bhopal night.

People Hear Alarms

The people in the shantytowns surrounding the huge plant heard the alarms. Many rushed out of their homes and up to the front gates of the plant. They thought there might be a fire, and they

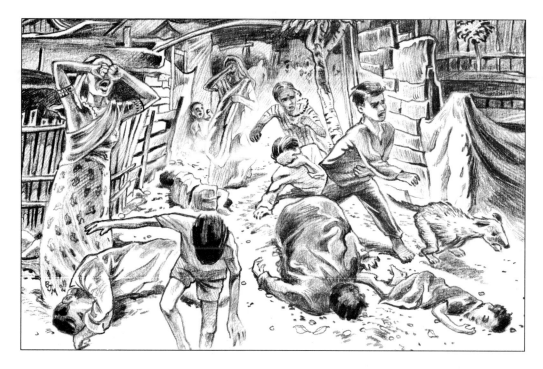

wanted to watch. These unfortunate spectators were overcome by the gas and were among the first to die. The gas continued to creep through the shantytowns. People sniffed at the air and wondered what the strange smell was. But they did not have to wonder too long. Out of the darkness, someone began to yell: *"Zahreli gas phut gayee, hum sab mar jayenge!"* ("The poison gas has burst; we are all going to die!")

The people in the shantytowns awoke to the smell of the gas and the sounds of people fleeing. Union Carbide employees living in the shantytowns felt terribly helpless. They recognized the smell of the deadly gas but did not have gas masks. At least they knew enough to grab articles of clothing or handkerchiefs, soak the cloth in water, and breathe through it. Then the employees, like everyone else in the shantytowns, gathered their families and followed one another into the chilly streets, making their way toward the city.

Deadly Cloud Followed Them

Groups of fleeing people trampled whatever got into their way. Those who fell were either stepped on or kicked aside. Most of the people ran south, toward town, but they were running with the path of the wind. The deadly cloud, hugging the ground, followed them. Within minutes of the leak, the groups of hysterical people converged and spread in one wide swath toward the railway station.

At the station, a train had just pulled in and travelers were being greeted by their families. They heard the siren from the plant, but they thought it was just a fire. They continued to talk and embrace, unaware of the danger. Some argued over prices with the porters checking their baggage. Others sat and talked at the coffee counters, while rickshaw drivers cried out for passengers. Suddenly, they heard the screams of the crowd passing by. Within seconds, the gas was upon them. People began to choke with every breath, their eyes and nasal passages burning. Horrified, they pleaded with Allah or other gods for help. In terror, men and women stripped off their clothes, thinking their nakedness would cool them and ease the choking sensations. Others clutched their necks and fell to the platform, their mouths oozing blood. The lively station had been transformed into a scene of death.

The panic increased. Another train arrived, filled with hundreds of passengers. Luckily, stationmaster H.S. Bhurve rushed out and waved to the train to move on. The train's shutters were closed against the winter cold, protecting the passengers from the gas. Bhurve's quick thinking saved hundreds of lives. After the train passed, people leapt off the platforms and onto the tracks, fifteen feet below, to avoid the gas. They lay sprawled in the dirt, with broken limbs and cut faces.

Everybody Stricken

Munnibai Balkishensingh, the water woman, was terrified. She had first thought that the harsh irritation she felt in her throat and eyes was from the chili powder a

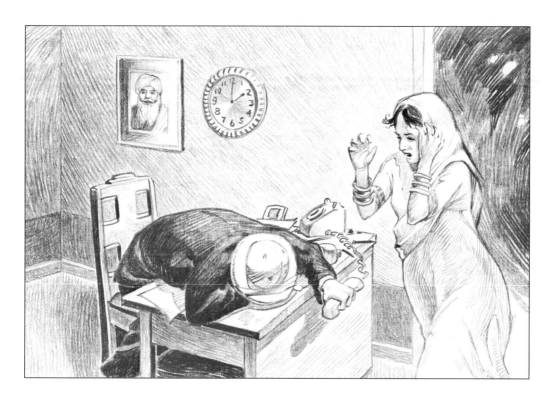

vendor was using on his omelets. But she soon realized that everybody in the station was stricken and whatever was in the air was killing them. She found the deputy controller in his office near the tracks. He, too, was suffering from the effects of the gas. She told him she needed to find the station doctor. The controller mumbled that he could not do anything: "Can't you see that I am also dying? We are all dying from the gas."

Munnibai left the controller's office and headed for the office of Bhurve, the stationmaster who had just saved the incoming train from tragedy. Perhaps he knew where the doctor was. Stepping inside Bhurve's door, Munnibai gasped. He was dead at his desk, the telephone receiver in his hand.

Munnibai left the station to search for the doctor's house. But she could not find it. Minutes later she returned to the control room, where she discovered the doctor dead inside the door. She ran out to the platform. In agony from the effects of the gas, she jumped off the misty platform and onto the tracks, where she knew there was a water tap. She bathed her face in the cool water. The sound of the water splashing on the ground caused others who were suffering to jump off the platform toward the sound, but most fell onto the tracks and were injured or even killed from the fall. Others, alive, climbed over the dead to get to the water.

Now Munnibai could see a little. She looked up at the platform. What she saw shocked her. Just minutes before, the atmosphere was joyous, with embracing and kissing and happy conversation filling the night. Now there was silence. Six hundred bodies littered the station, and about a third of them were unconscious or dead. Some were alone. Some were embracing. Some were mothers and fathers, with children in their arms, face down. Munnibai, in a daze, walked around the lifeless station. Finally, she went blind and collapsed.

Keswani, the journalist, had awakened, gasping for breath, at 1:30 A.M. in his home in Old Bhopal, about a mile from the plant. He felt he was suffocating. At first he thought the irritation in his throat was from a cold. But then he looked out his window and saw people running through the streets. He called the police. A gasping voice told him: "Union Carbide's tank burst! None of us will survive!" Keswani handed wet handkerchiefs to his family members and told them to breathe through them. Then he got his brother to drive some family members away on a motor scooter. Keswani himself got another scooter, put on goggles, and put his wife and fifteen-year-old sister on

the seat behind him. He drove toward the plant. His first thought was to go to the plant and kill its reckless managers.

"Where are you going?" screamed his wife. "You're going right toward the gas!" He stopped suddenly, realizing the danger, and turned the bike around, heading toward the city.

Chandabee awoke about 1:00 A.M., after a restless sleep. She felt sharp labor pains as she lay on her mat on the floor. Her throat and eyes hurt. She heard the crowds running and screaming outside. Her husband got up and grabbed her by the hand. It was hard but she had to run, with her husband,

her two daughters, and her mother-in-law. The pain in her belly was terrible, but she continued on, past retching and coughing people. Her husband had to drag her through the streets. Finally, she stopped. Sprawled on the ground, she felt she could no longer bear her intense pain. "God! I am dying!" she screamed.

Sayed Abbas, the television repairman, had traveled by train earlier that day all the way to Japalpur, several hours from Bhopal, and had returned home after midnight, exhausted. All he wanted to do was sleep. Now he lay on the mat in his bedroom, his eyes burning. He thought terrorists had thrown a

THE BACKUP SYSTEMS THAT FAILED

The backup systems in the Union Carbide plant in Bhopal, unlike the automatic backup systems at an identical plant in the United States, were manual systems. Any danger had to be spotted first by a technician and then reported; a manual backup system cannot recognize and respond to danger signals by itself. Here are the five major backup systems that failed in Bhopal on the night of December 2, 1984:

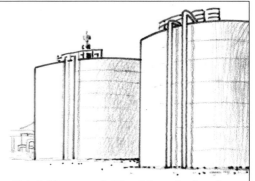

Third: The possibility of transferring the liquid to a nearby tank was ruled out because it contained some MIC already.

First: Spray from the fire truck hoses could not reach the fumes and neutralize the escaping gas.

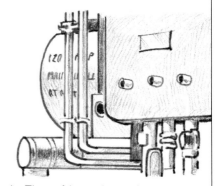

Fourth: The refrigeration unit under the tanks to cool the liquid had been turned off five months before.

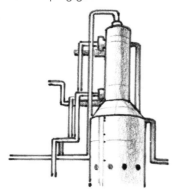

Second: The scrubber pump, a cleansing device used to pump caustic soda solution inside the vent gas scrubber failed to work. The soda solution would "scrub," or neutralize, the escaping gas and turn it into harmless vapor. Recently back from repair, the pump was either out of caustic soda solution or still defective.

Fifth: The flame tower, a ninety-foot high pipe used to burn gases in the air, was out of order.

bomb in the street, something that had happened before. But at 1:00 A.M. a neighbor pounded on his door and yelled: "The factory is leaking!"

Abbas gathered his family and went to find a rickshaw for his feeble mother. He ran out alone into the mob and found one. Abbas flashed his money—it was all his savings, but it did not matter to him now—and the driver took him back to the house. But when Abbas returned to the street with his mother, the rickshaw was gone. Someone else had taken it. Again, Abbas entered the throngs of people. Nearly blind, he got lost. He did not think he would ever find his way back to the house. Retching, vomiting, swept along with the people, Abbas began to panic. He reached the railroad tracks. He followed them, knowing they headed back out of town. Breathless, he fell several times. Finally, he fell and cut his face and hands. He began to lose consciousness. There were bodies near the tracks, all around him. He made one more effort to rise, to find his family, but the gas overwhelmed him. He collapsed on the tracks.

Stricken people began heading for Hamidia Hospital. People arrived cut and bleeding from falling in the streets. They were retching and vomiting, and their eyes were burning. Some arrived naked or wore shredded clothing. The first patients arrived about 1:15 A.M. By 2:30 A.M., there were four thousand people at the hospital. By noon the next day, just twelve hours after the leak spread, over twenty-five thousand victims covered the hospital grounds.

Four

The Suffering Continues

About an hour after Union Carbide workers abandoned the building, engineers from another company, Bharat Heavy Electricals, Ltd., secured the leaking tank. By that time, however, all the gas had escaped.

The deaths continued. Irritating the eyes and nasal passages of its victims, the gas crept into and inflamed the lining of lungs. This caused heavy fluid buildup in the lungs. Victims who were severely affected actually died from drowning. At the hospitals, autopsies were hastily performed to find out the cause of the deaths. Doctors cut open fresh corpses to discover cherry red blood, darkened lungs, and a bitter almond odor—all the signs of cyanide poisoning.

The surviving gas victims en-dured terrible suffering. About 80 percent of the adults and 50 percent of the children could barely breathe for days after the accident because of lung damage. More than 90 percent of the victims had chronic coughs. Nearly one-third of the Bhopal victims treated for lung problems suffered from lung fibrosis, a condition in which the lungs are unable to take in sufficient oxygen.

Death Statistics Varied

Varying statistics regarding the number of deaths surfaced. One reason for the different numbers is that countless bodies were "kidnapped" from the morgue by relatives in the early hours after the leak and quickly cremated, in keeping with religious beliefs. On December 5, three days after the leak, state officials announced that 1,267 people were cremated or buried. The Catholic agency Caritas said that 20,000 people died. More conservative estimates put the total deaths between 2,500 and 10,000.

The five area hospitals and twenty-two clinics, understaffed and overwhelmed, did their best to comfort the dying. At Hamidia Hospital, the scene was tense. Victims began arriving at about 1:15 A.M. Forty-five minutes later, with victims now in the thousands, journalists arrived at the hospital to find only one doctor, moving from one patient to the next, administering eye drops and handing out pills.

Soon, additional doctors and stu-

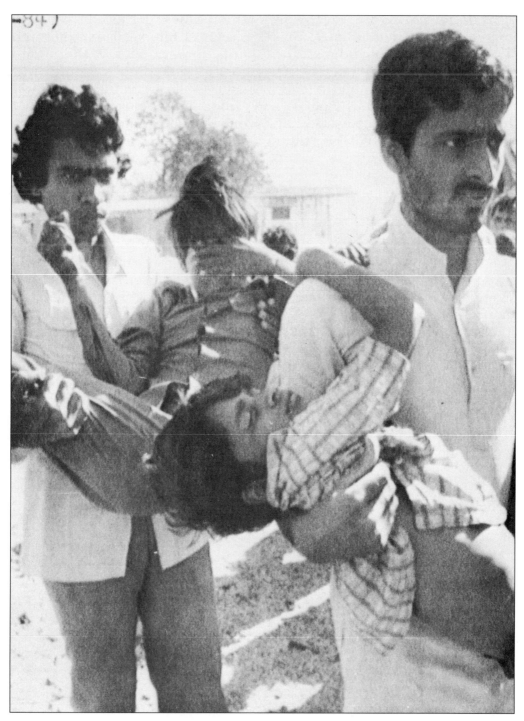

Two men carry children to a hospital for treatment of blindness. The children had been exposed to deadly gas that escaped from the Union Carbide plant.

dent doctors arrived. They were astounded by the number of victims sharing beds or crouching on the floor, begging for relief. They watched as husbands and wives ran up and down the halls, darting from one room to the next, searching for one another or for their children. They saw babies lying listless on cots, with feeding tubes stuck into their arms and oxygen tubes in their noses. The doctors immediately went to work. Harried and exhausted, they worked twenty-four-hour shifts, while all around them a seemingly endless flow of victims coughed, screamed, choked—and died.

At Hamidia Hospital, cadavers were being lined up outside on the lawn because of lack of space in the morgue. The morgue held most of the bodies gathered from the streets of Bhopal. There they were laid in rows on the floor, photographed, then covered with sheets to await identification. Unidentified corpses were piled, one on another, in corners. Among the bodies in one pile was Sayed Abbas. At about 5:00 A.M., this "corpse" awoke.

With great effort he pushed and pulled himself out of the pile of bodies that had kept him warm in the refrigerated room. Horrified at what he saw around him, he wrapped himself in a sheet and tried to get away as fast as he could. A police guard opened a door and saw Abbas, clad in a sheet, coming at him.

"A ghost!" the guard yelled. "Someone has risen from the dead!"

Abbas ran past him. All he could think about now was the safety of his family.

Bodies Lay in Rows

Shortly after the leak, three hundred bodies lay in rows at the railway station, waiting for a single doctor to decide which were alive and which were dead. He bent over each body, listened through his stethoscope, and ordered those with heartbeats into one truck and those without heartbeats into another truck. Munnibai had no perceptible heartbeat. She was placed in a truck and taken to a nearby crematorium, without having had the chance to be identified by relatives. This was done in such a hurried way because officials and doctors thought an epidemic of cholera might result if the corpses were not cremated immediately.

If a relative had come and recognized her body, Munnibai would have been placed on a single pyre of firewood. But since no one identified her, she was placed with other unidentified corpses for a mass cremation. She was placed head to toe in a row of about fifty corpses. A man spilled kerosene on the wood covering the corpses, then went to one end and lit a match. Instantly, the wood went up in flames. At that moment, a man who had come in to look for his relatives saw Munnibai's foot move.

Her foot was already on fire as the man rescued her and dragged her to safety. She was then taken to a nearby hospital to recover.

Chandabee and her family miraculously made it to Sultania Hospital, just east of Hamidia Hospital. But they were not admitted because the

Warren M. Anderson, the chief executive officer of Union Carbide during the Bhopal gas leak.

hospital was too crowded. She went with the others across the street to a little park where a truck driver picked them all up and drove them to a first aid center on the edge of town. There, unconscious, she gave birth to a baby boy. Her mother cut the umbilical cord with a stone, as she would have had they been back in their tribal village. When Chandabee regained consciousness and felt the baby at her breast, she vowed never to forget this day. It was a day of death but a day of birth, too. She named her son Gasmiya, after the deadly substance.

Luckily, Raj Kumar Keswani and his family were able to escape the fumes. In the days after the leak, he took no consolation in the fact that he had been right about the Bhopal plant.

The full horror of the disaster was perceived at dawn. Thousands of animal carcasses littered the streets. Trees appeared shriveled and yellow. Local authorities who went door to door found dwellers dead inside homes that had been transformed into locked, private gas chambers.

Mass Funeral Pyres

The shaken city slowly came to life. Construction cranes went into action, removing decomposing bodies of cattle and water buffalo from the streets. Some survivors mingled, while others began gathering the fly-covered corpses and assembling mass funeral pyres. Tailors, once busy repairing saris and dhotis, were suddenly overwhelmed by the demand for shrouds for the dead. Those blinded by the gas wandered and stumbled along in the quiet morning, searching for relatives and trying to comprehend the terror that had come to their city.

In the first few days after the disaster, the state government officials debated how to handle the arrival of Warren Anderson. Due to arrive on December 6, Anderson, the chief executive officer of Union Carbide in the United States, represented the company that had caused the death and suffering of so many Indians. The officials in Madhya Pradesh were naturally angry and wanted to take action

Workmen spray the tarpaulin covering the Union Carbide plant. They are attempting to neutralize the poison gas that may still be leaking from the plant. Several impoverished children from the neighboring slum stand in the foreground.

against Anderson and his company. Yet Union Carbide was a powerful force in India's economy, and government officials did not want Union Carbide to take its plants out of the country. After much discussion, the chief minister of Madhya Pradesh, Arjun Singh, decided to arrest Anderson.

Anderson Thrown in Jail

Upon his arrival in Bhopal, Warren Anderson was thrown in jail. He and two officials of the Bhopal plant were arrested and charged with "negligence and criminal corporate liability" and "criminal conspiracy." Under Indian law, the second of these charges carries a maximum penalty of death.

For several tense hours, Anderson and the plant officials were detained and guarded to keep crowds from getting near them. The crowds of citizens were extremely angry and might very well have bypassed a trial and given Anderson the death penalty themselves.

Pressured by central government officials in New Delhi, Singh allowed Anderson to be released on a $2,500 bond and flown to New Delhi, where those colleagues who had come on the plane with him were being held. Anderson contended that the company was not responsible for the deaths because the Bhopal plant was safe and identical to the ones in the United States.

After Anderson and the others were released, other Union Carbide officials wanted to reopen the plant

to get rid of the MIC liquid that still remained in the tanks. They feared that the remaining gas could erupt and cause another disaster. They also thought that the deadly cyanide could still be leaking into the air from the MIC storage tank, even as late as three or four days after the initial disaster.

The city of Bhopal was extremely angry and upset about Union Carbide's management and balked at the idea of letting these people near the plant. After the disaster, an attempt to storm the plant was made by several thousand Bhopal residents. Desperate to turn the hostile crowd away, the outnumbered plant officials and police told the crowd that another poisonous gas leak was occurring.

On December 10, local panic

DEATH BY DROWNING

The MIC gas irritated the lining of victims' lungs, causing pulmonary edema, a fluid buildup that decreases oxygen capacity. During edema, the fluid doubles the weight of each lung. Unable to bring oxygen into their fluid-filled lungs, victims suffered from excruciating pain before dying by drowning.

Others suffered from related maladies and disorders. Many experienced damage to their central nervous systems—arms and legs were rendered useless. Lack of oxygen affected the functioning of their brains, causing paralysis and loss of speech. Blindness occurred as the gas burned the eyes. In addition, these victims would suffer from weakened immune systems that would leave them vulnerable to a number of diseases.

Men, women, and children wait for a bus to leave Bhopal. Despite official assurances about the safety of the plant, these people demanded to be evacuated from the area.

grew at the announcement of the removal of additional gas from the plant. Fearing another accident, many residents demanded to be evacuated. Though reassurances were issued by Union Carbide and government officials, they developed a limited evacuation plan. Schools were closed and transportation out of Bhopal was provided for all residents who wanted to leave.

Operation Faith—the name given by Indians to the processing of the remaining MIC into the finished pesticide product—was put into action. Fifty Indian scientists supervised the process, which was successfully completed. The evacuated residents returned to their homes. Now they could attend to the business of counting and mourning their dead.

Victims Turn to Law

In their suffering, many Bhopal victims turned to the law. They wanted Union Carbide to give them money to compensate for their suffering and medical bills. The rumors of these suits brought American lawyers to Bhopal in what commentators called "the great ambulance chase." (An "ambulance chaser" is a lawyer who encourages victims of accidents to sue for damages and become his clients.)

The lawyers were a visible and sometimes thoughtless presence in Bhopal. They stayed in expensive hotels and ate dinner with Indian legal experts; they searched through

files and documents at relief offices outside the Bhopal plant, seeking potential clients. They claimed their motives were pure. Melvin Belli, a well-known lawyer from San Francisco, said, "I am here to bring justice and money to those poor little people who have suffered at the hands of those rich sons of bitches." But others saw the invasion of lawyers as little more than a hunt for a piece of the settlement. Said Illinois lawyer Carole Bellows: "It certainly reinforces the perception that lawyers are ambulance chasers."

Lawyers Want Trial in U.S.

The American lawyers wanted the Bhopal case to be filed in the United States, rather than in India. There were good reasons for this. One was that the outcome would be quicker if done in the United States. "If the suit were filed in India, the judgment would be in the next century," said Nani Palkhivala, one of India's prominent attorneys. Also, American lawyers were better trained in this kind of law involving civil suits for wrongful actions, called tort law. Therefore, both lawyers and victims believed the case would be better tried by American lawyers in the United States.

In the meantime, Union Carbide sent money to Bhopal in a relief effort. Among the payments the company made were one million dollars directly to the Indian government and five million channeled through the Red Cross. In India, the government initiated efforts to compensate the suffering victims.

People were paid 10,000 rupees ($830) for each dead member of their family.

In February 1985, two months after the disaster, American lawyers were consolidated into several groups by a United States judge. These groups represented the thousands of victims and would bring the main suit against Union Carbide. After the grouping process, the lawyers began to gather information about the disaster.

Lawyers for Union Carbide formulated a strategy to defend the company. Right after the disaster, Warren Anderson had been quoted as saying that "somebody has to say that our safety standards in the U.S. are identical to those in India or Brazil or someplace else. Same equipment, same design, same everything." Although this statement was later found false, Anderson was hinting at the strategy his company would use in court.

Union Carbide decided to blame the disaster on a worker, or a number of workers. This strategy has been used in industry on several occasions. For example, in 1986 there was a chemical accident at the Kerr-Magee Plant in Gore, Oklahoma. A spokesman for Dow Chemical, which owned the plant, commented: "In many of these accidents, the human element is the biggest problem. A lot of people say you have to add equipment. But you cannot make these things idiot-proof. You still have to properly train people, have proper procedures—and stick to them." In the Soviet Union in 1986, "six human errors led to the Chernobyl nuclear disaster," according to a spokesman of the Kurchatov Atomic Energy Institute. Companies and governments will often use this simple explanation to make it appear as if they were the victims of careless workers. In this way, they can often protect themselves from the great legal—and financial—claims of victims.

Lawyers for Union Carbide went further in their argument. They claimed the leak had been maliciously caused by disgruntled workers. In other words, the employees, in a conspiracy against the company, had caused the disaster on purpose.

Lawyers representing the disaster victims, on the other hand, claimed that Union Carbide was at fault because the Bhopal plant technology was inferior and inadequate. They asserted that the management of a company was responsible for the design of the plant and that the plant was dangerously designed.

Another argument made by the prosecuting lawyers was that the Bhopal employees were inadequately trained. In the four years prior to the disaster, nine out of the twelve original workers, all trained in MIC technology in the United States, left the Bhopal plant. Many of the remaining qualified workers also left for other jobs in India and the Middle East. By late 1984, only a handful of employees knew much about the plant and pesticide production. The inadequacies of Union Carbide's worker training programs were exposed. Recruits at the Bhopal plant had only a four-week

People sit in a tent in a temporary refugee camp set up to evacuate people from the area surrounding the Union Carbide factory.

crash course in handling MIC, instead of a year-long intensive study. This was because Union Carbide did not want to go to the expense of extensive training. Some operators, as workers later claimed, had even failed tests in MIC manufacturing processes but were nevertheless sent to work with the MIC. Many operators also lacked adequate safety training: for example, they understood neither training procedures nor the use of helmets and gas masks.

Poor Management

Why were there few well-qualified operators? One reason was that employees were dissatisfied with the working conditions at the Bhopal plant. Also, poor management resulted in high turnover. Employees were not offered promotions and were continually threatened by job layoffs.

These job layoffs led to lax enforcement of standards. For example, indicator readings to check and make sure machinery was running properly were taken once, instead of twice, an hour. MIC samples were checked for dangerous impurities only once every shift, not twice. Cost-cutting became policy, and with cost-cutting came acceptable negligence.

Author Paul Shrivastava points out that the Indian government, too, played a part in the disaster. It became clear in the pretrial hearings that the government's inspection procedures for the plant were inadequate. Indian state officials who were assigned to check the plant were mostly mechanical engineers with little knowledge of chemical engineering. In addition, the state's pollution control board had never even tested the plant for gas emissions. "We did not look into it much because there was no reason to think there was anything wrong," said Arul Kumar, first secretary in the labor ministry. In fact, the air and water pollution control board did not even have any instruments to measure air pollution. This meant that every year, with no questions asked, the Bhopal government granted a license to the plant. Although there was faulty equipment in the Bhopal plant, the most serious factor in the disaster appears to have been the negligence and low standards on the part of many.

In late 1986, nearly two years after the disaster, the case had still not gone to trial in the United States. At this time, the Indian government charged Union Carbide with negligence, brought murder charges against Anderson, and demanded $3.3 billion on behalf of about 520,000 claimants. If Union Carbide were forced to pay, the company could be destroyed. Anderson responded by saying, "It is unfortunate that right now Union Carbide and the Indian government are facing each other across a gulf as wide as the oceans that separate our two cultures. We have tried in many ways to bridge it and decided that for now at least, it is simply a fact of life." In November 1986, Warren

Young victims of the Bhopal gas leak disaster protest the settlement reached between Union Carbide and India.

Anderson resigned his post as chief executive officer of Union Carbide.

In February 1989, before the case ever went to trial, all legal maneuvers and negotiations were suddenly halted. An agreement was reached between Union Carbide and India's Supreme Court. Union Carbide agreed to pay the government of India a lump sum of $470 million by March 23, 1989. The money was to be distributed to victims by a special government commission. In exchange for this sum, the government agreed to drop all charges against Union Carbide, including the murder charges against Anderson. An American attorney who represented India said, "It's a fair and adequate settlement for the victims." But many Indians were upset. They thought that the sum was much too low. They blamed their own government for betraying them by accepting an inadequate settlement.

Five years after the disaster, Indians were still angry at Union Carbide. On December 3, 1989, the five-year anniversary of the gas leak, the police arrested about eight hundred people when they tried to hold a protest inside the vacant Union Carbide plant in Bhopal. "Down with Union Carbide!" the protesters chanted, as hundreds of police officers in riot gear stood by and watched. The night before, protesters had burned Warren Anderson in effigy. Before the settlement, court statistics had concluded that the gas leak killed more than 3,400 people and injured more than 200,000. In 1989, relief workers told reporters that people still die at the rate of about one per day from medical complications caused by the poisonous gas leak. Today, it is estimated that more than 8,000 people have died, with over 300,000 suffering from the effects of the gas.

Through these efforts, the impact of the disaster on the areas surrounding the plant has virtually vanished. The effects of the disaster on the victims, however, have remained. Of more than 200,000 people injured, 10,000 have sustained lasting injuries, mostly to their lungs. Twenty-five hundred survivors are expected to remain partially crippled by lung, nerve, and eye disorders for life.

Permanently Scarred

Among the victims who would remain permanently scarred both physically and psychologically was Sayed Abbas. After escaping from the morgue, Abbas was reunited with his wife and two sons. He and his family were suffering from the effects of the gas. Discovering black patches on one foot, Abbas went to the hospital. Doctors at first informed him that he had gangrene and that his leg had to be amputated. This operation was later found to be unnecessary. Next, his youngest son died. Abbas wondered if he were being punished for "abandoning" his son during the gas leak. A few days later, Abbas's mother, who had returned to her native village, fell ill. Abbas went and stayed with her until she recovered. Thinking his troubles were nearing the end, he returned to his home in New Delhi, only to find his wife in tears. Their eldest son, too, had died.

Abbas bitterly awaited the judgments of the legal suits. He had lost two sons. His wife and remaining

Five

Return to Bhopal

Since the fatal disaster, the area around the Bhopal plant has been renovated. One year after the leak, in the slum of Jai Prakash Nagar, right next to the Union Carbide plant, the physical evidence of the gas leak was gone. The Indian government had significantly improved these and other slum areas. Drains were installed, trees planted, and the worst huts were torn down. The government supplied fifteen hundred free housing units for homeless survivors of the disaster. Medical facilities, though meager by Western standards, had been greatly improved. Union Carbide had initiated and supported job programs to help workers who had been permanently handicapped by the gas. And the first psychiatrist ever seen in Bhopal opened up and started business, primarily working with the victims of the disaster.

Children who have gone blind as a result of the Bhopal gas disaster. Many people have suffered long-term effects from the gas leak.

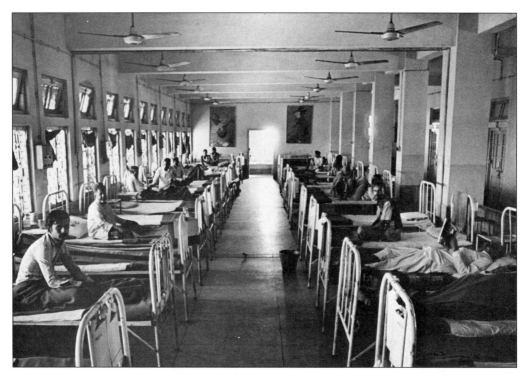

A year after the disaster, victims of the Bhopal chemical leak still suffer from ill-effects. Here, patients with continuing problems are seen in Hamidai hospital in Bhopal.

children were ill. He had difficulty with Indian bureaucrats and had not yet received any immediate compensation for the death of his children. His repair business was failing. The government was supposed to give him a loan to help him set up a television factory. He had no idea when—or if—the money would arrive. "I am a lucky man," he said, with sarcasm. "What else could happen to me?"

Munnibai's life, too, had been changed forever by the disaster. At the hospital, she had suffered terribly from the effects of the gas. She bled internally and could not open her eyes. She had pain in her burned foot. Her kidneys, chest,

and stomach also bothered her. Eventually, cancer was diagnosed. Doctors urged her to go to Bombay to seek treatment, but Munnibai said she did not want to die away from her children. Even when offered a trip to the United States by Union Carbide, Munnibai declined. She was concerned about the welfare of her family. She had to return to work. Nobody told her that gas victims too ill to work could receive their full salary. By innocently returning to work, Munnibai forfeited this right. Compounding her misery, her eldest son failed at school. She was determined, however, to send him back to school, to try once more so that he could someday find a better job, one that would make her proud. But not a job with Union Carbide. Of that she was certain.

Chandabee had been reduced to begging. But she had hope for her child, born out of death. She had not abandoned her dream of seeing her little son Gasmiya grow up to become more civilized than she. But her own troubles oppressed her. Suffering from injured lungs, both she and her husband could work for only a few hours. She spent the other hours of the day begging so that her family would not starve. Gasmiya, though, was awfully thin and it was not certain that he would ever walk normally. Chandabee's troubles were the same as those of many other people. The destruction of the gas leak had reached the next generation.

Even though it is too late to help the victims of the chemical leak, one positive change has occurred throughout India as a direct result of the Bhopal disaster. According to V.N. Kaul, the state's secretary of industry and commerce, the disaster had a great effect on environmental awareness. People in India have started to speak out against abuses to their environment. For instance, the state of Maharashtra sued the government over the pollution caused by an explosives plant. The state of Kerala sued a chemical plant for polluting a river. Villagers in Gujarat, who had been drinking polluted water for years, demanded and were granted a new source of fresh water. In Madhya Pradesh, the state in which the Bhopal disaster occurred, an India-owned petrochemical plant was forced to relocate to a less-populated area.

No Effect on India's Attitude

It is ironic, however, that this concern for the environment has not affected India's attitude toward multinational corporations. Since the disaster, foreign companies have continued to be invited in, and no technology has been turned away or turned down. In fact, according to Vijay P. Gokhale, the managing director of Union Carbide in India, "the government has gone even further, seeking ties with foreign industrial companies around the world, with the United States heading the list."

But how could the Indian people continue to allow foreign industry in their country after what had happened? Would not India be suspicious of multinational companies? There are many practical explanations for India's acceptance of these companies. For one, the Indian government, like other Third World governments, makes a lot of money by allowing multinational corporations to locate operations in the country. The corporations pay the host government for many services, including licensing fees and utilities use. Most important, though, is the offer of jobs. Union Carbide in India employed more than ten thousand people and was one of the highest-paying compa-

A slum-dweller fills water in front of the abandoned Union Carbide plant. Although life appears normal, thousands of people living in slums remain impaired by injuries inflicted by the deadly gas.

nies in India. Essentially, multinational corporations provide Third World governments with an easy solution to complex economic problems. Faced with an unhappy population suffering from poverty and joblessness, the host government knows a multinational can ease some of this discontent.

Another reason for India's continued acceptance of multinational companies is that people in Third World countries will often accept a higher level of risk than people in the United States, where industrial accidents are regarded as mistakes that must not be allowed to happen. Other countries are more fatalistic. Researchers from the International Labor Organization in Geneva, Switzerland found, for instance, that workers in a Volkswagen plant in Mexico tended to think of accidents as "fate" and relied on prayers to statues of the Virgin Mary set up throughout the plant as much as on safety training.

Regarding this acceptance of risk, author Fergus M. Bordewich had an interesting encounter with two men from the Bhopal slums, both of whom were severely injured by the gas leak. First, Bordewich spoke with Tunda Lal, whose lungs had been damaged. Lal, before the disaster, had worked as a mason for $1.50 a day in the slum of Jai Prakash Nagar when work was available. Now, as a registered victim of the disaster, he receives a substan-

tial settlement, along with many others. After the disaster and while waiting for the case to be settled, Lal begged in the streets. When asked what he would do if the Union Carbide plant were reopened tomorrow, with the same low-grade equipment and shortage of safety devices, Lal did not have to think about his answer: "If it opened tomorrow, I'd take any job they offered me. I would not hesitate for a moment. I want to work in a factory, any factory. Before 'the gas' Union Carbide was the best place to work in all of Bhopal." A neighbor, Tulsi Ram, leaning on a cane as a result of his own disability, echoed Lal's enthusiasm: "I'd go too, do or die."

High Risk Is Part of the Cost

Bordewich concluded that Lal and Ram, and others in Bhopal, throughout India, and all over the Third World, tolerate multinational corporations out of economic necessity. For them, high risk is part of the cost of seeking job security and fulfilling their ambitions. One can only conclude that when companies offer jobs, even at menial pay, to people in the midst of great poverty, a dangerous situation is often created. Unfortunately, many people desperate for work will accept hazardous job conditions. The likelihood of another disaster like the one in Bhopal looms large.

Glossary

flame-tower: a ninety-foot-high pipe used to burn gases in the air of the Bhopal chemical plant.

Madhya Pradesh: state in the center of India. Bhopal is located in this state.

MIC: methyl isocyanate, a deadly, colorless chemical compound produced at the Bhopal plant. It is one of the ingredients of Union Carbide's SEVIN, a powerful pesticide.

mosque: ornate temple where Muslims gather for prayer.

multinational corporations: huge corporations that operate worldwide, providing jobs and essential products.

pulmonary edema: a fluid buildup that doubles the weight of each lung. Left untreated, edema results in death by drowning.

rupee: a type of Indian currency.

sari: gown worn by Indian women.

shantytowns: urban villages made up of flimsy structures built by poor people.

squatters: poor people who live and build houses on land that is not their own.

Third World: the group of underdeveloped nations of the world.

Transmigration of Souls: religious belief which concerns the traveling of the soul out of the body.

tribals: lowest people in the caste system.

tort law: body of law covering damaging acts done by one individual to another which are not necessarily crimes.

UCIL: Union Carbide India, Limited.

untouchables: low class of people in the caste system. Only the Tribals are considered to be lower than the Untouchables.

varna: a class of people. Four varnas were established in Later Vedic Times. This was the beginning of the caste system.

vent gas scrubber: shaped like a rocket, the vent gas scrubber was part of the back-up system. It would receive any escaping gas and "scrub" or neutralize it with a caustic solution circulated by the scrubber pump inside it. In this manner, the deadly gas would be turned into harmless vapors.

Suggestions for Further Reading

Bordewich, Fergus M., "The Lessons of Bhopal," *The Atlantic Monthly*, March 1987, pp. 30-33.

Brata, Sasthi, *India: Labyrinths in the Lotus Land*. New York: William Morrow and Company, Inc., 1985.

Everest, Larry, *Behind the Poison Cloud*. Chicago: Banner Press, 1986.

Fishlock, Trevor, *Gandhi's Children*. New York: Universe Books, 1983.

Jones, Tara, *Corporate Killings: Bhopals Will Happen*. London: Free Association Books, 1988.

Kurzman, Dan, *A Killing Wind*. New York: McGraw-Hill Book Company, 1987.

Shrivastava, Paul, *Bhopal: Anatomy of a Crisis*. Cambridge, MA: Ballinger Publishing Company, 1987.

Weir, David, *The Bhopal Syndrome*. San Francisco: Sierra Club Books, 1987.

Works Consulted

Ashfaq, Ali, *Bhopal—Past and Present*. Bhopal: Jai Bharat Publishing House, 1981.

Chishti, Anees, *Dateline Bhopal: A Newsman's Diary of the Gas Disaster*. New Delhi: Concept Publishing Company, 1986.

Dunbar, Sir George, *History of India, from Earliest Times to 1939, volume one*. London: Nicholson and Watson, Ltd., 1949.

Iyer, Pico, "Clouds of Uncertainty," *Time*, December 24, 1984, pp. 24-27.

Iyer, Pico, "India's Night of Death," *Time*, December 17, 1984, pp. 22-31.

Morehouse, Ward, *The Bhopal Tragedy: What Really Happened and What It Means for American Workers and Communities at Risk*. New York: Council on International and Public Affairs, 1986.

Wilkins, Lee, *Shared Vulnerability: The Media and American Perceptions of the Bhopal Disaster*. Cambridge, MA: Ballinger Publishing Company, 1987.

Index

Kaul, V.N., 55
Kerala state, 55
Kerr-Magee Plant, 47
Keswani, Raj Kumar
  caught in gas leak, 34-35
  survives, 42
  warnings about Union Carbide plant, 27
Khan, Ashrat Mohammed, 22
Kurchatov Atomic Energy Institute, 48
Kuumar, Arul, 49

labor unions, 24-27
Lal, Tunda, 57
lawyers, 46-47, 48
literacy, 12
Lower Lake, 14
lung damage, 38, 44

Madhya Pradesh state, 10, 20
  arrest of Anderson, 42-44
  concern for safety, 55
Maharashtra state, 55
marriage, 17
methyl isocyanate (MIC)
  employee training in handling, 48-49
  in pesticide production, 22
  leaks from plant, 28, 30, 31
    cleanup attempts, 44, 46
    deaths and injuries from, 8, 32-34
  plant workers exposed to, 27
Mexico, industrial accidents in, 57
mosques, 13
multinational corporations, 23, 55-57

Nepal, 10
North Rajasthan Desert, 10

Old Bhopal, 10, 13-14, 18
Operation Faith, 46

Pakistan, 10
Palkhivala, Nani, 47
pesticides
  manufacturing of, 8, 18, 22
  use of, 24, 25
poverty
  in India, 10, 57
  scarcity of jobs, 15
  Union Carbide and, 17, 22
pulmonary edema, 44

Rajasthan Desert, 10
Ram, Tulsi, 57
Red Cross, 47
religion, 12-13, 17

SEVIN, 22
shantytowns, 17, 27, 30-31
Shrivastava, Paul, 49
Singh, Arjun, 44
slum colonies, 17, 18, 27
social classes, 14-15
Soviet Union
  Chernobyl disaster, 48
Sultania Hospital, 41-42
survivors, 9, 42, 52, 57

Taj-ul-Masajid mosque, 13
Third World
  multinational corporations and, 23, 55-57
tort law, 47
Transmigration of Souls, 12-13
tribal people, 20-21

Union Carbide
  Bhopal chemical plant
    backup systems, 24, 28-30, 36
    construction of, 9
    employee training, 48-49
    gas leak, 8-9, 28
      cleanup attempts, 44, 46
      deaths from, 8, 38, 44, 51
      effects of, 55
    rehabilitation of, 52
    safety failures, 22-27
    welcomed by residents, 17, 18, 22, 55-57
  chemical plants in India, 18
  compensation payments to India, 47, 51, 54
  lawsuits against, 48-51
United States
  chemical plants in, 24, 36, 44
  industrial accidents in, 57
  lawsuits in, 47
untouchables, 15, 16, 20
Upper Lake, 14

villages, 12, 15-17
Volkswagen, Mexico plant, 57

women, in India, 15

About the Author and Illustrator

The Author, Arthur Diamond, born in Queens, New York, has lived and worked in Colorado, New Mexico, and Oregon. He received a Bachelor's degree in English from the University of Oregon and a Master's degree in English/Writing from Queens College.

A former book editor, Mr. Diamond is the author of several non-fiction books. He is also an award-winning fiction writer. He now writes full-time and lives in Queens, New York, in his boyhood home with his wife, Irina, and their son, Benjamin Thomas.

The Illustrator, Brian McGovern, has been active in both fine art and commercial illustration for twenty years. His recent clients include AT&T, DuPont, Harvey's Lake Tahoe, and Chase Manhattan Bank. He has exhibited paintings in San Francisco and New York and was recently a published winner in *American Artists Magazine* in the "Preserving Our National Wilderness" competition. He has won several Best of Show awards in the fantasy art field and the 1987 Distinguished Leadership Award from American Biographical Institute in North Carolina.

Picture Credits